# Christian Parent Burnout

**Edith Lanstrom**

Publishing House
St. Louis

Scripture quotations are from The Holy Bible: NEW INTERNATIONAL VERSION. Copyright ©1978 by the New York International Bible Society. Used by permission of Zondervan Bible Publishers.

Verses marked TLB are taken from THE LIVING BIBLE, ©1971 by Tyndale House Publishers, Wheaton, Illinois. Used by permission.

Copyright ©1983 Concordia Publishing House
3558 S. Jefferson Avenue, St. Louis, MO 63118
Manufactured in the United States of America.

All rights reserved. No part of this publication may be reproduced, stored in a retrieval system, or transmitted, in any form or by any means, electronic, mechanical, photocopying, recording or otherwise, without the prior written permission of Concordia Publishing House.

---

Library of Congress Cataloging in Publication Data

Lanstrom, Edith, 1937—
  Christian parent burnout.

  1. Parents—Attitudes. 2. Parenting—Religious aspects—Christianity. 3. Parents—Religious life.
I. Title.
HQ755.83.L36 1983          649'.1          82-23671
ISBN 0-570-03897-9 (pbk.)

To Sig,
who walked the path with me

# Contents

|    | Foreword | 9 |
|----|----------|---|
| 1. | What Is Burnout? | 11 |
| 2. | Physical Symptoms of Burnout | 19 |
| 3. | Psychological Symptoms and Causes | 29 |
| 4. | Recovery | 39 |
|    | Epilog | 63 |

# Foreword

What parent has not been tempted to cry, "I give up! I just can't go on anymore. I'm worn out!"

Much has been written recently about professional people "burning out" at an alarming rate, some even taking the route of suicide out of their seemingly hopeless predicament. Sometimes the mind turns off from an emotional overload, and the victim pays the high price of a mental breakdown from which he or she may never recover.

Surprisingly, Christians are burning out too, and not just doctors, teachers, and ministers. Christian parents are also suffering the effects of burnout. Many don't know why they are burning out; many realize their situation too late; and the recovery, if any, is much longer in duration.

In this book Edith Lanstrom examines the experiences of Christian parents in order to understand what causes parent burnout, how it manifests itself, and some possible ways of dealing with it before it destroys the parent.

This is a book for *Christian* parents, since they suffer not only the typical effects of burnout, but they must also face questions of a guilty conscience, weakness of faith, and failure to practice forgiveness. One can be a Christian parent and still "burn out."

But there is a way out and back to normalcy. Attitudes and outlook can change, prospects can improve, relationships can be mended, forgiveness can do its healing work, and faith can revive hope.

—The Publisher

# 1. What Is Burnout?

As Carol helped Ted drag their staggering, vomit-covered 18-year-old son underneath the cold spray of the shower she wondered where she had failed. What had she done to cause him to become self-destructive?

Until the last year Carol had viewed herself as a successful parent, a mother who enjoyed the parenting role. In Rick's younger years there had been happy afternoons in the park, outings to zoos, and visits to amusement parks. As Rick grew older Carol and her husband had taken part in the scouting program. Many school years Carol had served as home-room mother. And she had lost track of the times she and Ted had volunteered to chaperon school dances and church youth-group socials. Rick had enthusiastically taken part in all activities until this year.

Now he defied his parents at every turn. Why? A few years ago the shouting matches that now were almost a daily occurrence would have been unthinkable. Carol hated them, but she often felt she started them. But as a concerned parent she felt she had to try to break her son's destructive behavior. If he couldn't see that his choice of friends and conduct were destroying him, wasn't it her duty to point it out?

Rick's loud objections to the cold shower startled Carol. Ted closed the shower door and they braced themselves for the next step of the oft-repeated scene. Carol knew that after Rick stripped off his clothes, he'd stumble out of the shower frantically trying to find a towel. She and Ted would help Rick dry off and then lead him to his bed.

Carol knew the rest of her night would be sleepless. And she would need physical and emotional stamina for tomorrow. It was the day of the annual church missionary society luncheon, and she was chairperson. But lately, organized church activities were becoming less and less relevant to her. The cheery nods, the smiling faces, the forced happy response only served to emphasize her aloneness among seemingly well-functioning Christians.

Jill hauled herself out of bed to stop the early morning squeals of her 3-year-old son. Perhaps if she reached him soon enough she could forestall the awakening of the baby. Mornings were difficult enough without both children demanding mutual attention. And trying to have a conversation at breakfast with her husband, Bill, was a romantic illusion. By the time Bill returned home in the evening, Jill found herself too worn out to be romantic or much of a conversationalist. Could she and her husband be drifting apart?

It had been another difficult day. Feeling completely exhausted, Marsha sat down at the kitchen table and poured herself a glass of wine. Perhaps it would numb her pain.

As she slowly sipped the wine she asked herself many questions: "How does a mother adjust to senseless physical and emotional cruelty suffered by her child? How can she help her child accept a reality she herself cannot understand?"

The treatment of her handicapped daughter, Anne, overwhelmed Marsha. It was fortunate that one of Marsha's friends had seen Anne's afternoon predicament and stopped to help her. On the way home from school, while hurling insults, several boys had pushed Anne into a muddy ditch. Marsha knew her daughter's heaviness, her uncoordinated condition made her unappealing to her peers. But was it necessary for other children to attack her? How does a mother answer a child's sobbing question, "Why, Mom, why? I wasn't bothering them." As Marsha got up from the table she uttered the cry of the father in Mark 9:24, "I do believe; help me overcome my unbelief!"

The soft low tones of the offertory did nothing to calm the rage within Cynthia. She glanced at her husband. Paul seemed lost in the peaceful sounds of the music. But it did nothing for her. Her mind could not concentrate on this music.

The words of the first hymn, "This Is My

Father's World," still bounced against the walls of her brain. Cynthia didn't see God in "rustling grass" or hear Him "speak to her everywhere." Cynthia wondered whether God even knew or cared about what was going on in her world.

Since her 25-year-old daughter and 5-year-old grandson had moved home six weeks ago, she barely had time to think or talk to Paul, much less commune with God! Most days she felt like a maid-servant to the rest of the family. It was as though the clock had turned itself back 20 years, and she again was having her schedule dictated by children's needs and by their school schedules. Every morning she had to get her daughter, Pam, off to an early college class and then get Rob, her grandson, ready for kindergarten.

Cynthia did not like this change in life-style. The past few years she and Paul had enjoyed a new feeling of closeness and freedom. Without children around they were able to do anything they wanted, any time they decided. Meal schedules were relaxed, their evenings spent doing what they chose. It was wonderful to be able to decide to do things on the spur of the moment. Now their daughter and grandson were dictating the pace of her life.

Because of Rob's morning kindergarten class Cynthia had stopped attending her morning Bible study. She felt the lack of this spiritual nourishment and missed the fellowship of her friends.

Cynthia had tried to tell Paul of her frustration, but he had glossed over everything by saying, "They won't be here forever." She knew Paul had the right attitude, so she tried to hide her feelings and make the best of the situation.

As the minister rose to begin the sermon, Cynthia forced her mind back into her present surroundings. Maybe she could glean one "sparkling spiritual gem" to soothe her resentment at having to defer to the needs of her daughter and grandson.

At three in the morning Phyllis and John found themselves sitting on the living room couch, weeping together. The events of the past eight hours seemed unreal. Last evening their unmarried college sophomore daughter had told them she was pregnant. How could this happen to them? To their daughter? Throughout her life they consistently had exposed her to Christian moral values, tried to set examples as moral parents. This development negated their efforts. They felt betrayed, used. Now Amy was turning to them for emotional support. Where would they find the necessary strength to sustain their daughter?

When it seemed as if they could shed no more tears, John took his handkerchief and gently wiped the dampness from his wife's face and then his own. Without saying a word he slowly went across the room and took the family Bible from the bookcase. He turned to 1 Corinthians and read one of their favorite passages:

> "Love is patient, love is kind. It does not envy, it does not boast, it is not proud. It is not rude, it is not self-seeking, it is not easily angered, it keeps no record of wrongs. Love does not delight in evil but rejoices with the truth. It always protects, always hopes, always perseveres."

John put the Bible down. Phyllis took one of his large, strong hands into both of hers.

"John, John, how can we endure this? I'm not sure my love or my faith is strong enough. All her life I've prayed for Amy, and look at the result."

"I don't know, honey. Let's ask God for strength to get through this ordeal."

Phyllis and John knelt by the side of their living room couch. John's husky voice indicated the hurting in his heart.

"Father, at this moment I don't feel loving toward my daughter. The pain of her betrayal cuts too deeply. But I know Amy must be suffering, too. Somehow, Father, inject Your healing spirit into this tragedy. In some divine way transform it into a blessing. As Phyllis and I struggle with accepting what seems unacceptable, hear our cries for guidance and strength. Protect the coming child that it may be healthy. God, help us to remember You are present in all of life's struggles. In Christ's name we pray. Amen."

John drew Phyllis close to him for a few moments of solitude. As they went upstairs to bed, Phyllis found herself wondering if God had heard their prayer.

The parents in the families illustrated here share three characteristics:
1. They are all burned-out parents.
2. Each feels isolated on his or her personal island of suffering.
3. All are Christian parents.

Yes, that's right. These caring, upstanding, church-attending parents are burned out, isolated from Christian support.

But what is burnout? According to Herbert Freudenberger and Geraldine Richelson, burnout is "to deplete oneself. To exhaust one's physical and mental resources. To wear oneself out by excessively striving to reach some unrealistic expectation imposed by oneself or the values of society" (*Burn Out: The High Cost of High Achievement* [Anchor Press/Doubleday], 1980).

Often, because of the burned-out parent's distorted perception, the tenets of his church seem too rigid. Or he feels guilt when he cannot measure up to self-imposed standards. For the enrichment of the church and the relief of the emotional struggle of the burned-out parent, it is imperative that the church shepherd these battered souls through this crisis. And it is through consistent person-to-person ministry that the spiritual and emotional dilemma of the Christian burned-out parent can be relieved and the desire for living rekindled. For the defeatist attitude of the burned-out parent will not allow him or her to acknowledge any positive aspects of his family life.

Christian parents do not burn out overnight, and there is often more than one contributing factor with which to deal. Combating parent burnout can be frightening, risky, introspective —painful. But when the challenge is honestly met, through the grace of God, it will result in unparalleled spiritual growth.

After realizing parent burnout is possible within the context of Christian life, the first step in defeating this 20th-century Goliath has been taken. Then if Christians will boldly explore this spiritually, physically, and emotionally draining phenomenon, a healing process can begin. And, at last, the Christian parent will feel free to approach Christian professionals and laity with his problems.

# 2. Physical Symptoms of Burnout

Christian burned-out parents are caring, idealistic, committed people. In fact, these sterling, selfless qualities are the reasons they burn out. In *Burn Out* Richelson and Freudenberger highlight this irony: "Burnout is pretty much limited to dynamic, charismatic, goal-oriented men and women or to determined idealists who want their marriages to be the best, their work records to be outstanding, their children to shine, their community to be better."

What's wrong with being an accomplished, functioning Christian person and parent? And how can an idealistic Christian parent who knows Christ rebuked His disciples for discouraging children from approaching Him be anything less than a conscientious parent?

He or she can't. In that case how does a person know when he or she steps over the line separating the conscientious parent from the burned-out parent? The first step in coping with this physical and spiritual crisis is to become acquainted with some of its symptoms.

Carol felt herself getting more and more irritated as she helped set the tables for the church luncheon. Younger mothers were happily sharing the latest antics of their babies, while the older moms were speaking in glowing terms of their children's academic and social accomplishments. As Carol worked she fumed inwardly. She listened with a smile plastered on her face, but she felt as if she were going to be sick to her stomach. She supposed that the combination of lack of sleep and worry conspired to make her feel this way. However, in the past few months this feeling of nausea had become a constant companion. Carol wondered what would happen if she suddenly stopped her work and screamed, *"Hey, ladies, cleaning up my son kept me awake part of the night, and worrying about him kept me awake until early morning!"*

They and she probably would be embarrassed. And the ladies would think of her as a real "weirdo."

Carol sighed, picked up the silverware, and went about her chores, wondering whether she fit into this group at all. Next month she would definitely skip this meeting.

As he struggled to put on his coat, Bill gave Jill a quick kiss on the cheek, tousled little Billy's hair, and with a "Bye, hon, have a good day" left Jill isolated on her island of boredom. Jill poked another spoonful of oatmeal into her baby daughter's mouth and then tried to reach down and encourage Billy to play with his trucks.

With some bitterness Jill remembered her youthful idea of motherhood. In her fantasy she would be well groomed and have breakfast started before her children awakened. When her husband came into the kitchen he would be greeted with an orderly family scene—wife serene and prepared for the day and enjoying a delightful children's conversation.

In reality she was lucky to get on her robe and slippers before one of the children's morning howls woke the rest of the household. Most mornings she was so busy getting the children fed that Bill had to fix whatever breakfast he could manage.

Jill did not like Bill to leave for work carrying the image of her as a harried, bathrobe-clad housewife. She supposed that she could set the alarm and get up earlier, but in her world what difference did it make how she looked? Reluctantly Jill admitted to herself that she envied Bill, envied his escape into a world that contained more than the drudgery of cleaning house, changing diapers, and doing the wash. And then she wondered how she could have had that thought. She and Bill had waited until both were well established in their careers before they decided to have children. And she had volunteered to stay home until the children were of school age.

What was wrong with her? She was committed

to a Christian marriage and to Christian parenting. But lately she felt her ongoing fatigue kept her from functioning well in either role.

She knew Bill thought they needed to get out of the house by themselves more often. But to Jill the effort involved did not seem worthwhile. Their one consistent joint outing was to church on Sunday. That one outing meant returning home to unmade beds and a cluttered house. In order to attend the worship service these household chores had to wait until afternoon. Bill was good about helping her, but the unrelenting demands of the children and the household chores left her worn out.

As Marsha stood in her kitchen reading the postcard reminder, she knew why she'd forgotten Anne's orthodontic appointment. She was sick of coping with all the appointments and trials of her handicapped daughter's life. Anne's 13 years had consisted of varieties of appointments: physical therapy; psychological, neurological, medical doctors; speech therapists. None of these had been able to erase or really define her daughter's nebulous neurological problems.

Years of struggling with the inherent problem of rearing a handicapped child had caused Marsha to think of the childless years of her marriage as "freedom days," days that were not burdened with responsibility. During that period she and Doug often, on the spur of the moment, would go to a movie, camping, or perhaps for a long drive. But that spontaneous lifestyle was in the past. Anne could not cope with sudden schedule changes. She had to be prepared in advance for any special outing or event. And Anne's world was Marsha's world.

Somewhere in the Bible she recalled Jesus saying, "I have come that they may have life, and have it to the full." Marsha wondered how that applied to her.

Although she had been a Christian all her life, it certainly did not overflow with anything but drudgery. It was made up of one dreary, taxing day after another, with no relief in sight. And these days her back ached constantly. Marsha opened the refrigerator, poured herself a glass of wine to sip while fixing dinner. It would relieve her backache. Then with another glass at dinner perhaps she could get through another evening of her daughter's slurred speech, her awkward movements, her accentuated learning difficulties.

Cynthia filled the ice pack, unplugged the phone, stretched out on her bed, and placed the ice pack on her head. Perhaps if she closed her eyes and rested for a little while she could get over this headache. The morning had been torture. She had awakened with one of her almost blinding headaches. Since she managed to perform her breakfast chores efficiently, neither her husband or Pam had become aware of her problem. And Rob was always happy as long as Grandma was around to supervise his bath, get him fed, and send him off to school on time.

Paul had no patience with her headaches. Since they started a month or so after Pam and Rob had moved in, Paul felt the headaches were due to tension. And a doctor's visit and tests had confirmed his opinion. When she told Paul that the doctor agreed with him he had rather smugly answered, "I told you so. Now just relax and get back to your old energetic self." She'd never again let Paul know she still suffered from these pounding attacks.

In the soothing quietness of her bedroom Cynthia could feel the tension seep out of her body. Even through her headache she appreciated this respite from a day made up of never-ending chores and errands. Hopefully the headache would be gone by the time Rob was out of school. She'd take him with her on errands. But they would have to hurry. She needed to get home and start supper. These days supper had to be finished early so that Pam could be free to study.

Pam was finding returning to college a demanding, time-consuming experience. Cynthia hoped that next semester, with improved study habits, her daughter would find schooling a little less taxing.

Cynthia took a deep breath and tried to relax. She really did want to get rid of this headache!

As she wrote the check for the wedding invitations Phyllis questioned if she and John had made the right decision. Their daughter, Amy, wanted to be married in the church, so she and her husband had consented to a small church wedding. If the marriage failed, though their daughter's reasoning would be faulty, Phyllis and John did not want to give Amy the opportunity to say a bad beginning had doomed it.

Dragging herself out of bed was an almost impossible task these days for Phyllis. Each morning, after a night of tossing and turning, she would get up exhausted and move robotlike through programmed days of ordering invitations and of fittings for the wedding dress, smiling and appearing happy.

She had hoped her daughter's wedding would be a time of closeness, sharing. Instead it was a time of alienation. Amy surrounded herself with her friends. When she was alone with Phyllis, she avoided eye contact.

Amy rattled on and on about inconsequential things. Phyllis thought by talking Amy hoped to lessen the awkwardness of the situation. But her daughter's magpie chatter got on Phyllis's nerves. She wanted to take her by the shoulders and shake some sense into her. Phyllis doubted Amy appreciated the seriousness of her marriage and pregnancy. Every time she tried to talk to her, Amy would answer in a disgusted tone of voice, "Don't worry, Mom, I can take care of myself." To

Phyllis, Amy's pregnancy obviously refuted that statement.

Now, to make things even more unpleasant, Phyllis found herself with an unshakable cold. And she was the one in the family who was never ill. She hoped she'd have the stamina to get through the wedding.

The onset of physical symptoms indicates that the continually beseiged parent is in the first stage of burnout. The most commonly shared symptom is bone-weary fatigue. For caring parents wear out as they try to meet all the physical and emotional needs of their offspring, an impossible task.

Fatigue may be a legitimate complaint when a couple is in the throes of raising young children. And the fatigue is accentuated by the repetitiveness of the days—one pressing chore after another: diapers to be changed, children to be bathed, children to be fed.

However, as children enter adolescence, a parent's fatigue can be a reaction to his or her children's rejection of the parent's value system, often interpreted as rejection of the parent himself.

Today's more lenient attitude toward divorce also contributes to parent burnout. Frequently, just as older parents are getting used to a more relaxed life-style, a divorced offspring with a child (children) will appear on their doorstep.

As followers of Christ the loving parents feel they have no choice but to welcome their son or daughter and his or her child (children) into the family fold. After all, it was Christ who rebuked His disciples when they discouraged children from approaching Him. "Let the little children come to me, and do not hinder them, for the kingdom of God belongs to such as these" (Mark 10:14).

And the sensitive, caring Christian can feel caught in a gnawing trap whose cutting edges are sharpened by the clash between his Christian beliefs and his human needs. And unless the parents and the returning child work out realistic guidelines for this new way of life, there can be backlash.

As parents unconsciously become entrapped by this gratification-of-children syndrome, they often develop migraine headaches, ulcers, hypertension, nervous stomach, or colitis. It is easier and more socially acceptable, and less painful to the psyche, to develop these kinds of illnesses than it is to work through the pain of changing warped spiritual and emotional concepts.

The discomfort of these physical problems may force the parent to consult a doctor. If this professional is sensitive to his patients' needs, he will spend time trying to find the underlying causes for the health problems. Hopefully, the doctor will have enough perception and training to help his patient through this rough passage.

Often the doctor will recommend some type of counseling. It would be ideal if the Christian parent would seek out a minister or a Christian counselor. This would allow both the client and the therapist to work within a framework in which both are functioning or trying to function.

If, for whatever reason, the parent is unable to obtain professional help, an empathic Christian friend can be supportive by walking through this crisis with the suffering friend.

Once a parent decides to seek counseling or to share his or her troubles with a trusted companion, a giant step into the heart of the conflict has been taken. In this skirmish the parental casualty rate will be high, as the soul searching, at times, will be almost unbearingly painful. But the discarding of warped perceptions will make the struggle worthwhile.

# 3. Psychological Symptoms and Causes

Burned-out parents feel they have lost control of their lives. To them, their lives and their children's lives are careening down an emotionally destructive track which stretches unendingly ahead, offering no options. It is difficult, almost impossible, for the well-intentioned Christian parent to accept the idea that rebelling or troublesome children's behavior cannot be controlled or changed by them. And as parents realize they cannot control their children they find themselves questioning whether God really is in control of anything.

As Carol put Rick's jeans in the washer she wondered whether she would be sticking them and her son under a cold shower again this weekend. At least Rick limited his drinking bouts to the weekends. But why did he have to drink at all?

Countless times, trying not to sound judgmental, Carol and Ted had explained to their son the physical damage alcohol could do to his body. It had proven to be useless. Rick automatically rejected any advice.

In an effort to break their son's destructive

behavior they had tried confining Rick to home territory over the weekends. But the first weekend he was not grounded he would resume his drinking. For her own sense of well-being, Carol questioned whether the weekend "homing technique" was worth the effort. Throughout the two days Rick would make cutting remarks to her and her husband. And they always carried the same message of resentment: "I can't wait until I finish school in June. The only reason I'm sticking around here is to get that high school diploma. It'll help me get a job, so I can escape my prison and my prison guards, you two."

Daily Carol bombarded God with prayers to rid her son of his alcohol addiction. At times she would almost demand God remove this ugly, piercing thorn from the heart of her family life. Obviously God had not heard her prayers, or He would have lifted this demoralizing burden from her shoulders. But why did God not hear her anguished supplications?

Negative thoughts crept insidiously into Carol's consciousness. Carol began to think that because she was a Christian, God should have answered her prayers and cured her son's addiction. It was obvious to Carol that God did not care or that He had no control over Rick's behavior. She felt herself and her family rejected by God. Carol stopped praying and wrapped herself in a bitter, resentful cocoon. Nothing made sense anymore.

Jill saw her children as two clever puppeteers who masterfully pulled the strings of her life. If she needed to go anywhere she had to schedule her trip between naps, feedings, and other responsibilities. And the days she had errands scheduled the puppets would invariably change their daily habits, causing her to rush through her activities or to abandon them altogether. This was a constant source of irritation. When working, her days had been organized, orderly. She had been an efficient office manager. But now no matter how well she planned her day, the two little puppets would somehow manage to disrupt her schedule.

Sewing used to be her favorite hobby, but she hadn't even opened the sewing machine in more than a year. When Jill had been the mother of one child, she had tried to sew a few times, but even then she never managed to complete a project. There were too many other demands on her time: household chores, trips to the park, doctors' appointments. Jill wondered whether her life would ever again function smoothly.

Jill viewed herself as a slave to her children, with no options for changing. She felt she had lost control of herself and her children.

Marsha came out of the doctor's office feeling more depressed than when she had entered it. In a private conversation with the doctor she had told him she felt Anne had shown no positive physical or emotional change since her last checkup. In fact she thought Anne's personality was daily becoming more abrasive.

The doctor assured Marsha he could see minor changes in Anne. But because of her neurological problems, her physical and emotional growth patterns would have to be measured in inches, not miles. In his opinion years of mistreatment by her peers had bruised Anne's psyche, leaving deep scars. The social ostracization, along with her medical problems, had contributed to Anne's developing defensive personality. The doctor pointed out that Anne's entry into her teenage years could be traumatic enough without additional problems. The doctor felt some of Anne's obnoxious behavior was typical teenage conduct, exaggerated by her physical and emotional problems.

Driving home Marsha fumed within herself. She had gained absolutely no comfort from that visit. As far as she could tell, there was no improvement in Anne, no matter what the doctor said. All she could see or hear was an overweight, sloppy, uncoordinated daughter, whose argumentative nature and health problems never ended—just went on and on—growing wildly like unhealthy weeds.

Before Anne's birth Marsha had envisioned God as a kind, merciful Father who would stand by His people and not give His people burdens they were unable to bear. "Well, God surely wasn't standing by me and helping me past my troubles," Marsha brooded. And she had just about reached the limit of her physical and emotional endurance. Why didn't God realize that? She kept crying out to Him for relief, but He chose to ignore her. Often Marsha felt as if she were a worn rag doll whose limbs were being painfully torn from her by her handicapped daughter —a condition she was unable to change. Why didn't God help her out?

Paul watched Cynthia's slow mechanical movements as she buttered the breakfast toast. A year ago she would have been scurrying about the kitchen, preparing breakfast and breathlessly telling him of her activities for the day. Or she would have been asking about his workday schedule. But since Pam and Rob had moved into the house Cynthia had lost her vitality.

Paul wondered how having family move back home could so radically change an adult personality. Again and again he reminded Cynthia that this was only a temporary arrangement. And his wife would always answer in a flat monotone voice, "Yes, Paul, I know." Her eyes were dull and her face blank. Her lack of emotion made Paul feel as if he were talking to a robot that was incapable of expressing feelings.

He knew, in order to care for Rob, Cynthia had given up all outside interests. And he was sure being tied down with a small child would cause some resentment. But whenever he encouraged her to talk about her feelings she would say that everything was fine and there was nothing to talk about.

Paul wished that Pam and Rob did not have to live with them, but he saw no alternative. Pam could not support herself and Rob until she finished her degree and had a marketable education. He and Cynthia would have to be economically and emotionally supportive of their daughter. Why couldn't Cynthia accept the situation?

Paul ached for a revival of the former close, loving relationship with his wife.

Phyllis peered at the luminous numerals on her bedside clock—3 a.m.—and still sleep evaded her. Slowly, carefully, so as not to wake John, she got out of bed, put on her robe and slippers. Maybe a cup of warm milk would induce sleep. She flipped on the family room light and her eyes gravitated toward the small maple buffet, where a collage of Amy's childhood pictures stood. Slowly Phyllis plodded over to the buffet and picked up her daughter's pictures. What innocent joy these photographs portrayed—Amy the toddler, snuggled in her father's arms, Amy the 8-year-old ballerina, Amy, smiling and laughing down from her favorite oak tree. The recalling of those sunshiny, carefree days painfully flooded the guilt-ridden crevices of Phyllis's mind, causing accusatory tears to sting her cheeks.

With tears cascading down the front of her

robe, Phyllis collected the pictures and hid them away in the bottom drawer. Her battered heart could not stand to look at the innocence in her daughter's face, a trusting simplicity Phyllis knew never could be recaptured.

As she drank her warm milk Phyllis tried to analyze where she had erred in raising Amy. Where had she failed? What had she done wrong? She thought she had thoroughly explained the facts of life to her daughter. And when Amy and her soon-to-be son-in-law started dating steadily, she again had a frank talk with her. Although Phyllis did not condone premarital sex, she believed she realistically had dealt with the moral attitudes of the day. While she told Amy of her personal moral stand, she also had informed her daughter about available contraceptives. Amy had assured her that premarital sexual relations were not part of her value system, so she would have no use for this information.

Now she knew Amy had been lying to her. Why? Because of Amy's inability to face her own conduct? Because Amy did not want to risk her parents' disapproval? Was this pregnancy an act of rebellion? Phyllis wondered where her influence had been lost.

And she felt trapped by her daughter's irresponsible action. If she managed to get through this wedding she would retreat into a private shell of her own, shutting out a hostile world. With a deep sigh she placed her empty cup in the sink and started back upstairs. As she slipped back into bed she directed a plea to God, "Enough, enough, already. I can't take any more."

Burned-out Christian parents have lost all hope for positive change in their children's lives or for any improvement in family relationships. They feel they are swirling around in an uncontrollable whirlpool of child-induced stress. And how did it happen?

After all, their children were being raised in a Christian home, exposed to Biblical teachings. And in Eph. 6:1 doesn't it say, "Children, obey your parents in the Lord, for this is right." But as children rebel against their Christian parents, and as these parents at times want to disown their children, the situation seems to become unmanageable.

The anguished parent frequently views his powerlessness as unique, one not acceptable in his definition of the well-adjusted family. This distorted perspective can cause the parent to remove himself or herself from the orbit of Christian families whose inner dynamics seem to be functioning well. Burned-out parents don't need a painful reminder of their feelings of incompetency.

Isolation is a psychological symptom and a contributing cause of parent burnout. In their aloneness these aching parents magnify the tiniest flaw in their perfectionistic image. They constantly question past actions. "Should I have been lenient? Was I too demanding? not demanding enough?"

And because they are not having any intimate relationships with other Christian parents, their feelings of inadequacy can easily overwhelm them. Negative psychological concepts force them to see themselves as unacceptable beings. And if they are not acceptable to themselves, how can they possibly be acceptable to God?

In today's society, when it is frequently necessary that both parents hold jobs outside the home, parents trying to be "Super Christian Parents" can, without much effort, become victims of parent burnout. For at the end of a long, exasperating day, working parents can find that shifting their emotional gears to mesh with the moods of their children is an impossible task. Their fatigue may cause words to be spoken more sharply than intended, resulting in a three-ring circus of agitation.

And at the end of such a stressful day how might the parents feel if they read Eph. 6:4? "And now a word to you parents. Don't keep on scolding and nagging your children, making them angry and resentful. Rather, bring them up with the loving discipline the Lord himself approves, with suggestions and godly advice" (TLB). Guilty! These parents would feel too guilty, too emotionally frayed to remember the warm, strengthening moments of family life—shared outings at a park or beach or an evening at the pizza parlor. Their ability to cope has reached its snapping point.

Traumatized parents sometimes find it easier to bury their feelings, to emotionally withdraw from a situation, than to risk sustaining more hurt. An uninvolved person cannot feel pain. Unfortunately this flawed technique will shield a person not only from pain but also from joy.

Loss of control, isolation, self-induced guilt, physical and emotional exhaustion, withdrawal, resentment toward God, all are common symptoms of the burned-out parent. By-products of these symptoms may be alcoholism, loss of intimacy with loved ones, and even divorce.

Operating from the most unselfish, loving mode, the Christian parent unintentionally can confuse his identity with that of his child's. And this overidentification with children and their accomplishments, or lack of them, is a basic problem of parent burnout. The parents' intense involvement with their children causes them to lose their own identity and their own sense of self-worth. A crisis is inevitable. But how do these combat-fatigued parents come out of their traumatized state?

In most cases a burned-out parent's own sense of aloneness, defeat, and unacceptability will not let him or her turn to the church for comfort. But he or she may turn to an open, nonjudgmental friend or in some cases a counselor.

# 4. Recovery

Carol wanted to pick up her phone and cancel the bowling date. Why had she accepted Mary's invitation? True, a few years ago she and Mary had enjoyed bowling on a PTA team. But Carol felt her family circumstances had changed so radically she could not enjoy the company of "normal people."

What would she have in common with them? After all, she was the parent of an alcoholic. And Mary was the well-adjusted mother of two successful sons, one an outstanding high school achiever, the other a second-year student at a prestigious university. To Carol, Mary's life ran smoothly. Mary bubbled with vitality.

Carol sighed. At last the bowling game was over, and she had successfully maintained a facade of happiness, managing to smile as if she had no worries.

On the way home Mary made a suggestion that cracked Carol's carefully constructed bravado.

"Why don't we stop for a bite to eat and then maybe browse through the stores for a while? It's great to have some free hours."

To herself Carol admitted she had nothing pressing on her afternoon schedule. And her stomach did feel a little less queasy than usual. Maybe a carefree afternoon would be fun. With her heart quivering, Carol agreed to spend the next few hours with her friend.

As Carol and Mary chatted companionably over their second cup of coffee, Mary confessed that having her college-student son home practically every weekend was driving her wild. She and her husband thought their son was enrolled in the college of his choice, doing what he wanted to do. Instead their overly conscientious, academically oriented son was coming home every weekend, dumping all his insecurities onto their shoulders. And they resented it.

Yet they were afraid not to be a sounding board for their son because they were concerned about his emotional equilibrium. Both she and her husband were encouraging him to transfer to a less demanding school or perhaps to attend the local community college for awhile. Of course, their son viewed either of these suggestions as an admission of failure on his part. Mary confessed she felt as if she were walking a tightrope.

Because of Mary's open, vulnerable attitude Carol risked asking a question.

"Mary, when you are so concerned about your son, how do you maintain your positive air, your vivaciousness?"

Mary chuckled. "I try to do things, like bowling, that take me out of the house and get my mind off my son and his problems. And I pray a lot."

"Mary, do you really pray a lot? And, if you do, do you think God hears your prayers?"

In a soft, earnest voice Mary answered, "Carol, I really do pray a lot. And every morning I try to have private devotions; I read material I think will help me cope.

"In the past six months I have found myself reading and rereading the Book of Job. He certainly had his trials and tribulations, but eventually he learned to trust God for his strength. Daily I have to work at trusting in God's strength and not my own. I guess as a mother I want to take control, solve all my child's problems, but I can't. And it is with conscious effort I try to hand my son's emotional difficulties back to God.

"Devotions, prayer, associations with fellow Christians sustain me in this battle. That is one reason I go to church. Continuing Christian support makes the term 'enabling faith' a real thing to me. This shared Christian fellowship emphasizes our mutual commitment to Christ, our Savior. It makes it possible, it enables me to face daily problems, knowing in all circumstances He is there."

Carol felt long-held-back tears slowly furrow down her cheeks. "Mary, I'd like to tell you about my problem . . ."

In the late afternoon as Carol prepared dinner she pondered her friend's words. With some alarm she remembered she had told Mary she would go to church this coming Sunday. Quite unexpectedly Carol found herself praying.

"Lord, help me to realize that Rick has to recognize and face his alcoholism himself. As he struggles with his problem may I be a caring, supportive parent but never a problem-solving mother. With your help Rick will have to overcome his addiction. Father, please meet Rick at his point of need. Infuse him with Your strength, enabling him to become an emotionally whole person.

"O Lord, daily walk with me as I strive to become more trusting. As my family walks through this valley, God, never let me forget You are there.

"Thank you for Mary. Through her faith I am once again being brought closer to You. Lord, Lord, let me not again become blind to Your ever-present strength. All this I pray in Christ's name. Amen."

Jill watched the well-groomed woman walk into the park. Hanging onto her baby's stroller was a little girl who looked about her own son's age. Jill was curious about the age of the baby in the stroller. Noticing the infant propped up with small pillows, she guessed the baby to be about three months old.

How could the mother of two young children manage to have a neat appearance? It was all she could do to gather up the kids' bottles and get to the park for a few hours of relative calm. There was no time for herself. As Jill watched the woman walk toward the playground, she was conscious of her own faded jeans and shirt and her hastily brushed hair. Guilt pricked Jill's conscience, reminding her that before the birth of the children she had always been well groomed. To herself Jill admitted she might have a few spare moments in the evening, but she was so exhausted all she wanted to do was go to bed and get some sleep.

Suddenly Jill realized the woman was going to sit down beside her. Just her luck. As the woman sat down a deep sigh escaped her lips. Jill wondered why. Nothing suggested defeat, discouragment. A question abruptly brought Jill back from her reflections.

"How old are your children?"

"My boy is three and the baby is six months."

As she spoke Jill judged the stranger to be about the same age as herself, a "thirtyish" mother. Was that the reason she had chosen to sit on this bench?

"My little girl is three also, but my baby is only four months."

As the other mother spoke, Jill noticed she had reached into a large denim diaper bag and pulled out a banana.

"Is it all right if your son shares a banana

with my daughter? By the way, my name is Jean Bowman."

Jill glanced at her son, whose attention was captivated by the newest member of the younger set.

"I'm Jill Kelso. My son would be delighted to have part of your daughter's banana. How thoughtful of you to offer."

Jill watched as Jean peeled the banana, discarded the peeling in a plastic bag, and threw it in a nearby trash can.

"Actually, it's a case of self-preservation. Maybe your son will take my daughter under his wing, include my child in his play group. That way I can have a few moments for adult conversation."

Without thinking Jill replied, "I know exactly what you mean. My days are spent talking in 'childrenese.' When the children are grown do you think we'll be able to converse in adult language?"

Jean countered with a smile and asked, "Do you think we'll have to take a course in adult language?"

Jill giggled at the absurdity of the idea. Her new-found companion continued the fantasy.

"Maybe the city recreation department would include it in their classes, or maybe the YMCA would take it on as a project. Or maybe a new school devoted to the retraining of babbling mothers could be founded."

While the babies slept and the children played, Jill and Jean continued visiting, exchanging names and background information. The settling of children's arguing was smoothly handled as the burdens of mothering began to be shared.

That evening Bill was very grateful for this "Jean person." When he came in from work he found Jill with her cheeks glowing, her eyes sparkling with an intensity he had not seen in over a year. After putting the children to bed, even after her busy day, Jill joined him on the couch. And for the first time in months Jill asked about his workday. They were communicating! Bill felt a lightness of heart.

After talking over his work situation, Jill rapidly told Bill of meeting Jean and then went on with more amazing information. She told Bill that one morning a week, for a nominal fee, Jean left her children at a child-care center located in her church. Some mornings Jean said she would go home and wash her hair or sew. Other times she would go out for a cup of coffee and for shopping. This escape time permitted Jean to renew her acquaintance with herself. And this revival of identity refilled her coping well, enabling her to better meet the demands of her two young children. She had invited Jill to drop off the children at the church next week.

In an exciting bubbling voice Jill rushed on.

On another morning she and Jean were planning to attend an exercise class at Jean's church, putting the children in the same center. The center's attendants played educational games with the children and, more importantly, lavishly administered large doses of tender, loving care. Would it be okay with Bill if they attended Jean's church this Sunday?

Without hesitation Bill answered yes. To himself he acknowledged that he would willingly attend any church whose outreach so effectively revitalized his wife. Besides he wanted to meet this ministering angel named Jean.

Marsha hummed as she fixed Anne's Saturday lunch. She was thinking how much her life had changed since her first appointment three months ago with Dr. Holt. And as she reviewed her first visit with him she smiled—she had been so nervous. Remembering, she was again aware of Dr. Holt's compassion.

At first she had wondered whether it had been wise to call Dr. Holt. But after all, he had been a close friend of her parents for years. And during her teenage years his family and her family had gone on many outings together. And Dr. Holt had lovingly united her and Doug in marriage. Since this special person had performed their marriage ceremony she and Doug had always thought of their wedding as uniquely meaningful. How could a union so lovingly entered result in the havoc which surrounded her today?

Marsha recalled that after pulling into the church parking lot she had hesitated going into the church building. Only the hopelessness of her situation had made her continue.

When he saw her standing in his study door, Dr. Holt had instantly put her at ease by embracing her in a warm, fatherly hug.

"Marsha, how good it is to see you. I've only been here a week and I'm still like a fish out of water. It's a blessing to see a familiar face."

This compassionate act had caused Marsha to dissolve into tears. While it embarrassed Marsha, it did not seem to disturb Dr. Holt. He gathered up Kleenex from a box on his desk and wiped her tears.

Vividly Marsha remembered their conversation: "I'm sorry, Dr. Holt. I guess I'm more uptight than I thought. Please forgive me."

"Marsha, Marsha, don't apologize for tears. They can relieve pressure. Do you feel like talking about what's causing these tears?"

"Oh, Dr. Holt, everything is wrong. You do know Doug and I have a 13-year-old daughter, Anne, who is handicapped. Although she's not mentally retarded, she is emotionally immature, physically unappealing. Her problems occupy most of my time. In the morning I wake up exhausted, dreading the day. At night I go to bed exhausted, dreading the coming day."

"Marsha, your parents told me you had a handicapped child. I'd imagine coping with this drains a person. Have your parental duties made you and Doug give up your favorite sport, tennis?"

47

Marsha answered with an emphatic yes. "Anne takes all our extra time."

"Do you think not allowing yourself any enjoyable, fun activity could be contributing to your exhaustion?"

"I don't know, but I am too tired to think of playing any tennis."

Dr. Holt had noticed the smudges under Marsha's eyes. The rigidity with which she sat in the chair, the gauntness of her face suggested she was under much tension.

"Can Anne be left alone?"

"Yes. But we try not to leave her alone too often. She doesn't have any friends. Doug and I are her friends as well as her parents."

"This weekend, why don't you and Doug take time out to bat around some tennis balls. I think you might find it refreshing. I've noticed there are a number of tennis courts in this area. Why don't you try some fun tennis. I know to ease my burdens I find it necessary to have some sort of physical activity every day.

"Besides that, I find daily devotions center my life, help me maintain a balanced perspective. Through devotions and prayers I am able to keep my eyes focused on the cross. Marsha, let me give you a devotional book."

From his study shelf Dr. Holt took a small book and handed it to her.

Marsha glanced through the book, noticing

the months divided into days. It wouldn't hurt to give it a try.

"Marsha, I remember you used to be an avid reader. Do you ever allow yourself an hour to relax and luxuriate in reading a book, a magazine?"

"Very rarely."

"I wonder if you are ignoring your own needs? Even Christ urged His disciples to get away to themselves [Mark 6:31-32] and [in Matt. 14:22-23] even Jesus found it necessary to be alone. 'After he had dismissed them, he went up into the hills by himself to pray. When evening came, he was there alone.' Marsha, sometimes you can stand the battle only if you withdraw and commune with God. It allows you to renew your strength. Let something else go, give yourself free time.

"By the way, when I saw your name on my appointment calendar I called Jane, who insisted you and Doug come over for dinner Friday evening. How about it?"

Marsha started to shake her head, but Dr. Holt raised his hand.

"I won't take no for an answer. You wouldn't want me to get my neck wrung, would you?"

To her amazement Marsha found herself laughing.

"Oh, no, never. But I can't imagine Mrs. Holt making such a threat."

"Oh, no?

"Come on, Marsha. It's lunchtime, and you

and I are going out to celebrate the renewing of friendship."

Visiting with Dr. Holt had certainly changed her life and redirected her interests. For the past three months she and Doug had been meeting another couple for a Saturday morning game of tennis, and they went out to lunch together after the game. The physical exertion and the normal, enjoyable companionship relieved the stress of living with a handicapped child. And Anne had developed a sense of pride in being able to handle a lengthy time by herself. Most often she just watched TV and then, at noon, ate her lunch. But it gave her some sense of independence.

As Marsha recognized the significance of that thought, tears rimmed her eyes. A few months ago she would not have left Anne alone on Saturday. Thanks to Dr. Holt's encouragement she had dared to leave Anne, and as a result her daughter's self-esteem had improved. Somehow the time away from Anne diluted Marsha's feelings of resentment. Now she and her daughter shared a more acceptable relationship.

Marsha knew how fortunate she was to be able to confide in Dr. Holt. She and Doug were even attending church again and were thinking of attending a small Bible-study group.

Dr. Holt's realistic support amazed Marsha. Yesterday he had called to tell her a psychologist would be offering group counseling for parents of handicapped children. He also said that she had made him crucially aware of the extreme stress with which parents of handicapped children live. Dr. Holt believed this group would aid in the lifting and sharing of this burden. He had told her sessions would be held at the church one evening a week. He wondered if she and Doug would be interested in attending.

Of course he knew they would. Just anticipating the group sessions seemed to lift Marsha's burden. She put Anne's lunch in the refrigerator and went to put on her tennis togs. Another good day coming up.

Barbara checked the coffee cake in the oven. It was about done, and it looked good. With a sweeping glance she gave the kitchen a once-over inspection. Everything looked fine—place mats, silverware, napkins—and the little bowl of daisies in the center of the table added a welcome touch to the cheery, yellow room. The rich mellow odor of coffee told her it was perking. Quickly she turned, opened the refrigerator to make sure the bowls of fresh fruit were chilled and ready to be served. They looked inviting and delicious. She hoped Cynthia would think so too.

Convinced that everything was in order, Barbara sat down in a kitchen chair, let out a deep breath, closed her eyes and prayed,

"Father, please don't let my actions be upsetting to Cynthia. You know they are motivated by my love and concern for her. She's been withdrawn, tired, worn-out looking lately. Lord, I believe she's traveling down a path that I've already traveled. If it is possible, let me guide her away from this damaging route. Infuse this morning's visit with Your Spirit that it may help my hurting friend. O Lord, use me as Your instrument. All of this I ask in Your Son's name. Amen."

Cynthia parked her car in front of Barbara's house and, for a few minutes, let her head rest on its steering wheel. She needed time to compose herself. This morning had been a whirlwind. It had not been easy getting everyone off and her most pressing chores done before getting here.

And if she'd had a choice she wouldn't have come. But Barbara had threatened to come and get her if she didn't show up. That would have been worse! These days her house always looked cluttered, and she didn't want her friend to see that. It was kind of Barbara to invite her over for coffee, but she wondered why.

Barbara and her husband, Matt, had lived in town only about a year. When Cynthia and Paul had attended their church's couples club socials, they had become friendly with them. But in the past few months, since she and Paul were not attending the meetings, they saw them only at Sunday morning services. What on earth would they talk about this morning? Cynthia felt stale, out of touch.

It had been a delightful 30 minutes. The two women had compared notes on making coffee cakes. As Barbara poured another cup of coffee she asked casually, "How are things going in your family? Hopefully better than when we were in the same situation."

In spite of the hot coffee Cynthia turned cold. To cover her agitation Cynthia took a long slow swallow of coffee. Then she risked questioning her friend.

"What do you mean? I know you have three married children, all living away from home."

"Yes. They are now. But four years ago our oldest daughter and her 6-year-old twins moved back with us for two years. My daughter also had to go back to school. The resulting stress almost caused me to lose my husband."

Dismayed, Cynthia put down her coffee cup.

"You mean Matt? Barbara, he's head over heels in love with you. That's hard for me to believe!"

"He loves me now, and he loved me then, but I withdrew from him. Matt seemed to adjust to our family togetherness better than I. And I resented it. After all, I was the one who bore the extra burden of everything. The one who did the extra laundry, fixed the extra meals, cleaned the extra messes, adjusted her schedule to fit everyone else's. I felt as though I were nothing more than a slave!

"And I felt guilty about my resentment, so I didn't express it but drew more and more within myself. I felt no one cared about me as long as I performed my expected tasks."

Barbara watched Cynthia, trying to interpret her friend's reaction. Cynthia sat perfectly still, listening intently.

"About eight or nine months after our daughter and children had moved back, Matt began coming in later and later on Friday evenings, and I could tell he'd been drinking. Then quite frequently he began staying in town late during the week.

"Eventually, in desperation, I talked to our pastor about my dilemma. In addition to praying with me about the problem, he made some concrete suggestions. He suggested Matt and I make Friday night our 'date night.' Even though our daughter would be tired from her school schedule we deserved a night to ourselves. And she might enjoy a quiet, companionable evening alone with her children.

"The week before our first 'Friday date' I called Matt at his office and asked if he'd like a date with an exciting, new woman—me! I think he was taken aback but delighted. So we started our Friday night courtship. Sometimes we would go to a nice restaurant, sometimes to a hamburger place and, if the weather was nice, sometimes we would picnic. Cynthia, it was such fun!

"And always during the evening Matt and I were communicating. I learned Matt and I shared frustrations and resentments about our daughter's return home. And it helped dilute the emotions by sharing them. We also set up some guidelines for our daughter and grandchildren. After eight-thirty at night we were not to be disturbed unless there was a catastrophic emergency. Having that exclusive time together is how we survived those stressful years."

"How did your daughter and grandchildren react?"

Barbara smiled. "At first our daughter and grandchildren tried breaking through the new line of separation. But Matt and I were firmly united, and they couldn't make either of us change our mind. After about a month they accepted the new set of rules and everyone got along better, with more private space."

"Barbara, this wasn't a spur-of-the-moment invitation, was it? You wanted to help me avoid the same problem, didn't you?"

"Yes, I prayed that you would not be offended but would realize that I care and I am concerned about you."

Cynthia got up, went around the table and gave her friend a quick hug.

"O Barbara. Thank you. I am miserable. Let me tell you about it . . ."

Even after three weekly counseling sessions Phyllis found it hard to believe she was seeing a therapist. But when her cold had developed into bronchitis she had been forced to see her family doctor. In his office she had broken down and sobbingly told him of Amy's predicament. At that point the doctor had recommended counseling. Still, if her insurance had not covered the cost, Phyllis wondered whether she would have opted for this type of help.

But the sessions had enabled her to gain some insight. At least now she understood why she had put away Amy's childhood pictures. Through the counselor's skillful techniques Phyllis was able to realize she was experiencing an intense form of grief. She was grieving for her daughter's lost innocence—a childlike quality which, to Phyllis, Amy never again would possess. The naive character of their relationship was now in the past.

As she got in her car and headed toward the counselor's office, Phyllis wondered what insight she would gain during this session.

During the hour the therapist asked Phyllis if she believed in forgiveness.

Automatically Phyllis answered yes. After all, she was a Christian, and didn't Christianity incorporate that belief?

The doctor answered, "This weekend I read the story of the prodigal son. I wonder whether Amy could be a prodigal daughter?"

"You mean, doctor, like the prodigal son, Amy should be welcomed back into the household with open arms?"

"I don't know. How does that feel to you?"

"It feels horrible. I've been a concerned, loving mother. Why should she have done this? It goes against my values. And also she lied to me—even while I talked to her about premarital sex. She said she didn't believe in it. All the while she was taking part in it."

"Maybe she couldn't face her actions herself. Obviously you are having difficulty forgiving her. Do you think she is having difficulty forgiving herself?"

During the session, the question of forgiveness was never settled. Did she or did she not believe in forgiveness? All her life she had been a Christian. Central to this faith was a belief in forgiveness. Didn't Jesus say to forgive seventy times seven (forever)?

And didn't Paul say to the Ephesians, "Get rid of all bitterness, rage and anger, brawling and slander, along with every form of malice. Be kind and compassionate to one another, forgiving each other, just as in Christ God forgave you."

For days and nights Phyllis wrestled with the meaning of this Scripture, finally coming to the realization that she felt much bitterness and anger toward her daughter. But even as she waged her tormenting spiritual battle, she heard the rest of the passage—"forgiving each other, just as in Christ God forgave you."

Phyllis felt humbled when deeper spiritual insight broke through her tribulation and she recognized the unfathomable magnitude of God's love. He let His Son die on the cross to remove all guilt from penitent sinners. Beginning to understand this divine act permitted Phyllis to forgive her daughter and to reach out to Amy with unconditional love.

But Phyllis wondered whether Amy would be able to relate the significance of Christ's death on the cross to her particular dilemma. Phyllis prayed that her daughter would come to realize all she had to do was to confess her sin and ask for forgiveness through the redeeming love of Christ. And her sin, her guilt would be blotted out by the sacrificial love of Christ, the Savior—Amy's Savior. And Phyllis knew that if Amy experienced the forgiving love of Christ it would let her reach out with forgiving love toward others. Daily Phyllis prayed for Amy to realize Christ's accepting love was always available for just the asking.

At her next therapy session her counselor gave Phyllis a book on stress, *To Bend Without Breaking,* by Mary Ella Stuart. In her book Mrs. Stuart states, "Quite naturally, I am responsible for my children until they are old enough to assume more and more responsibility. When they are grown I am no longer responsible for them but rather to them."

Phyllis read and reread that statement. Ultimately she accepted the fact that she had been a responsible parent. Both she and John had nurtured their children in a loving home, a home in which Christian values were emphasized.

And though she still prayed her daughter would experience Christ's redemptive love she knew Amy, as an adult, had to be responsible for her choice and its consequence. With the facing of this reality the separation of identity had begun.

When the church recognizes the problem of Christian parent burnout, it must be treated not as an unacceptable aberration but as an oozing spiritual and emotional wound that can be healed by the acceptance of oneself through Christ.

It is a slow, arduous process to bring the Christian burned-out parent back into the mainstream fellowship of the church. In most cases, because of low self-esteem, the sufferer will not seek refuge in the church family. A burned-out parent can be intimidated by the impersonal organization of the institutional church but perhaps will feel less threatened by a one-to-one relationship.

During his ministry Christ met the needs of many people. In Mark 8:1-10 Jesus was concerned about the hunger of people who were about to start a long homeward journey. So miraculously, using seven loaves of bread and two fish, He fed a crowd of 4,000. In the story of the woman at the well (John 4:4-26) Jesus in an open, caring manner, met a Samaritan woman at her point of spiritual need. He fed her, not with bread and fish, but with spiritual water that would forever satisfy her thirsting soul.

Following Christ's example, a concerned Christian must be willing to meet the burned-out parent at his or her point of need. This may mean letting the bruised parent see that a Christian, whose life is undergirded by a strong faith in the love and goodness of God, also suffers through periods of doubts and depression.

But the exposing of one's weaknesses must be coupled with the revealing of Christ's redemptive love as a Christian's ever-present source of strength. Initially the helping Christian's service may have to demonstrate this belief.

Often this demonstration will have to be of a very practical nature. In the service of Christ a person can find himself or herself baby-sitting, cooking a meal, doing the grocery shopping, mending clothes, mopping a floor. Many times a person will find himself just listening to the burned-out parent's distressing story. It is vital to be a nonjudgmental, empathic listener. Some churches conduct "active listening programs" for lay persons.

As a more trusting relationship between the parent and the counseling friend develops, it will seem natural to talk of Christ's agape love.

And through the commitment to the following of His way the concerned Christian has helped to heal a wounded member of Christ's church. In the union both persons have grown. The ministering one has developed a more compassionate understanding of the Christian burned-out parent. The parent has learned to accept his vulnerability. He now recognizes the words of Rom. 3:23-24: "All have sinned and fall short of the glory of God, and are justified freely by his grace through the redemption that came by Christ Jesus." Acceptance through Christ frees these parents to accept themselves as perfectly whole, wonderful creatures of God. And in accepting themselves they develop their own separate identity, which frees their children to develop their God-given abilities.

Then the ministering Christian and the healed Christian can hold up their heads in confidence, each knowing he has fought the good fight, he has finished the course, he has kept the faith.

# Epilog

This book was written as a ministry from one Christian burned-out parent to another. It is my prayer that it will open the door for investigation of the Christian parent burnout phenomenon within the loving, caring context of the church. I know it is needed. I am Amy's mother.

Edith Lanstrom